Table of Content

Preface

Congratulations on picking up a book on time management! It does not matter which book you select from amongst the *thousand* books available in the market; you decided to commit to learning time management, and that is worth being appreciated and congratulated! And better yet, you decided to learn this invaluable skill from a book, rather than reinventing the wheel! You value your time and decided not to waste your precious time experimenting with techniques and beating around random places looking for answers to your problems. And let me tell you – You are in the right place!

I value and respect the time and effort you will spend reading and practising this book, and I promise you will get the return you desire. Every line of this book is written with a purpose; you will not find one stray line throughout the book. The book sticks to its point and is made as precise as possible, without compromising on the quality of the information and examples given. This way, you get only the information you seek, and you will get it fast! All the techniques have been summarised into bullets after each chapter with a book summary at the end of the book to ensure you will not have to re-read chapters to remind yourself when you are ready to take action.

One thing I want to promise you before you get into the book – learn all the principles, take action, and you will return from the book as a different person! A person with total control over his time and a person not troubled by time management ever again! That's a promise! All you need to do is read and take action!

PART I: Restructuring Your Stream

Chapter 1

Why Time Management Does Not Work!

Panting and out of breath, he thrust the last plank into the ground. The sky had turned orange, and the day was coming to an end. He stared at his work standing tall in the shadows of the setting sun. A proud smile escaped his tired, wrinkled face.

"It's all gonna be fine now! I am making good progress...." he murmured.

Ralph called it a day and went home to his wife. He stole a glance at her but was quick to realize the heat of the morning argument hadn't died out yet. All she wanted was a shed in the backyard to keep all the garden tools. After an hour of dialogue in the morning, old Ralph gave in and gave it a shot. He visited a dozen sawmills in town that morning until he was confident he had enough wooden planks to build the walls of the shed. He took them all to his backyard and got to work. He intended to finish the walls of the shed before he got to the roof, so he thrust the planks into the ground one by one. By the time he put down the 6th plank, the 1st one fell to the ground.

"Ha! A weak plank, you stay right there on the ground as you deserve," he convinced himself as he moved on onto his next plank.

As Ralph lay in bed, he made a plan to finish the roof first thing in the morning. He was confident of what he had accomplished and woke up motivated to finish what he had started. But the morning didn't go very well for the poor old man. He was shocked when he stepped into his backyard - The shed was gone! All his work was gone! The planks he put down hadn't survived the night; they weren't strong enough. All the planks lay flat on the ground, just like the plank that gave up on him the previous day.

Ralph felt defeated! All his work had gone down the drain. He was confused on what he did wrong to deserve such punishment.

"I can't believe it…. It's all gone… and it's all because of her! Why can't we just store the tools in the front room! Why do we even need a shed?" his raspy voice thundered as he stormed into the house to have another dialogue with his wife.

So, what are your thoughts on old Ralph? He wasn't very smart, was he? What if I told you that you probably have made the same mistake?

A person trying to learn time management is very similar to old Ralph. He collects his tips and techniques from various sources; he thrusts them into his schedule. He finds it hard to fit them in but gives it a shot. After a while, the planks start falling. He convinces himself the fallen tips weren't of much use and carries on to thrust in the other tips. At the end of the day, he feels productive and good about himself. But soon, he forgets half of the tips, gives up on some, and finds the rest unsuitable. He makes up his mind that time management doesn't work and concludes he does not need it. He was doing fine without it.

From my very own experience, there are countless blog posts, videos, and books that provide countless time management tips and tricks, all covering various fields and some even contradicting each other. You read these various tips and tricks, you try to apply it in your life, and before the day ends, you probably have forgotten about them. Don't get me wrong; these sources have amazing life changing information, but there is something critical they are missing, something too huge to be explained in a blog post or video, something that can be explained only through a seminar or a book. So, what is this "secret"?

The Secret to Productivity That Lasts

Imagine a scenario where Ralph had dug a few deep holes, stuck a few strong logs of strong wood in them, covered them in concrete, and continued to build the shed on them. The shed would have been complete, and Ralph would've suddenly found it useful. How could Ralph even think of making a shed without laying down a foundation? It's the same deal with time management. You need a strong *foundation* to put your tips on – you need a strong *time management system*. This is the "something" that all tips and tricks miss! You need to build a foundation before you thrust various techniques into your day.

Let me validate my point further with a real-world example. Brian Tracy, one of the best time management experts, teaches something called "positive affirmations." According to this technique, we repeatedly say a positive sentence to ourselves to rewire or recode our brain. If I want to become an excellent time manager, I would say – "I use my time well, I use my time well" a few times until my brain accepts that I am a good time manager. If my book was a tips book and I give this as a tip, you would probably apply it. But how is it going to help you? You would say it out loud and your brain will accept it, but how are you going to manage time well if you do not know how? It could be golden to a person who already has a system in place; for others, it's like trying to convert ocean water into gold. (Did you know ocean water has 20 million tons of gold in it? But in a diluted inaccessible state.)

What Is a TMS?

Whether we know it, all of us have a system of going through our day. Imagine your day as a stream of water. It originates every morning, flows through the mountains of tasks and obligations, the dark valleys of stress and pressure, along the sunset in the plains of relaxation and breaks only to be born again the next morning. In the simplest possible way, you can describe your stream as – waking up, working, spending time with loved ones, and going to bed. These are the activities that make up your stream. You do it on a routine basis to sail through your day. When you try applying various time management tips and tricks, you are trying to remove the detours of your stream by building obstructions in its path. Your stream, with all its strength of years of repetition, can easily break through your obstructions to return to its original path.

We can't contain the stream with obstructions, but we can dig a whole new route for the stream – a more efficient, smoother, and faster one. The new path is the "*time management system.*" It is a serious restructuring of your stream, using various time management principles to find the best suited route for your needs! Once you build this route, you can follow various tips and tricks to make sure your stream stays on the right path. The tips now get a new and better meaning. They become the guardians of your stream as the stream is already in the right path. The "planks" have something to sit on!

A System for Life

Now, why should you do all this? You can see it in the title of the book– to create a long-lasting system – a way of living that will last a lifetime, a system that will make you an efficient and productive person, rather than just being efficient and productive at work, a system that will manage your time while you work or have fun, a system that will take care of your time without you having to worry about it. Yes, it is possible and you too will have your very own system by the end of this book with which you can stop worrying about time and focus on things you could do with your time.

The purpose of this book is to help you build your own personalized time management system (TMS), a system specifically built just for you! Hence, I won't be narrating a single system for you to follow. I would rather fill your mind with the ingredients and elements of a good TMS, so you can create your very own personalized system. In the first part of the book, I will guide you through creating a TMS. In the second part, we will set up some safeguards and solve common problems you face on the journey. It does not matter if you are new to time management or if you have prior experience with time management. The book can help you create a solid new time management system if you are a beginner and will help you tweak, reengineer, or even rebuild your time management system if you have a routine in place. (I will have a <u>TMS action sheet</u> at the end of the first part, which you can follow to create your own system.)

I would like to take the privilege of skipping the "why manage time" or "importance of managing time" topic. It seems to be a staple in every time management book. You have your reasons to manage time, or you wouldn't pick up this book. You need time management to succeed, live life happy, become rich, and all those things.

So, let's get into more serious discussions – changing your mindset.......

Chapter 2

Mindset: Dig a New Path

- Success is 80% mindset and 20% mechanics.

- Anthony Robbins

It All Starts with You!

The biggest truth of time management is "Time management has nothing to do with time." You read that right! Time flows! You can't stop it nor can you control it. I could probably make you stick to the book by giving fake promises of increased time and less work, but the truth is – time management cannot reduce your responsibilities nor can it give you 48 hours a day. I know it is not something you expect me to tell in a book like this, but fads aside, you know it, too! Let's go with practicality, rather than going through magical methods to preserve time.

You have your unending responsibilities on one side and your limited time on the other side. When neither are willing to budge, the only thing that can change is the thing between. Time management is aimed at you! Not your work, not your time but you! Time management trains your brain to do things the best way possible to finish them quickly. This can free up time for your personal life or for more work. So, let's create a healthy mind before we get into the mechanics of the book.

- You cannot control what happens outside you, but what happens within you is a 100% under your control.

- Stefan James

One Lesson to Change Your Life

Allow me to deviate a little from our topic to come back stronger than ever. This is arguably the most important part of the book, so read on with utmost attention. This one lesson can change your life for good. It did for me. I am sure it can do so for you, too....

In a research conducted in 1998 in the *Case Western Reserve University*, a few participants were selected and split into two groups. One group was asked to eat white radishes while the second group indulged in warm oozy chocolate. They were then given a puzzle to solve. The participants weren't aware the puzzle was unsolvable and had no known solution to it. It was observed that the radish eating participants gave up sooner on the puzzle, while the chocolate group continued and tried longer to find a solution for it. No, I am not talking about the benefits of eating chocolates, but of a phenomenon known as "ego depletion." It took the radish eating participants some amount of willpower and discipline to choose the radishes over the chocolates, even though the former is healthier. This reduced their willpower, which led to them giving up quicker on the puzzle.

Researchers have proven willpower and self-discipline are exhaustible. One has a limited amount of willpower a day. Every decision you take, be it big or small, is a toll on the willpower. Think of it as the fuel in an aircraft; once the fuel empties - you crash. Why else do you think great people like Steve Jobs, Mark Zuckerberg, and Barack Obama wear the same colored clothes every day? They intend to reduce their fuel usage as much as possible to apply it to more important tasks.

So, how do you use your limited willpower? – create powerful habits! 95% of what you do every day results from habits, good or bad. Do you want to work for long hours without a break? – create a habit. Do you want to wake up early and be productive? – create a habit. Do you want to exercise every day? – create a habit. Do you want to be organized in life? – create a habit. Once you are habituated to doing something, it takes considerable willpower NOT to do the same. Deny a runner his morning jog and it will break him down.

How to create a habit?

You create new habits by using your willpower! The problem is – most people use their willpower to push themselves to work out or wake up early or to stay organized. It won't be long before you empty your tank and give up on the task. You need to use your willpower to create a habit of working, rather than using it to do the work. You just need enough willpower to "start a habit." It takes the most willpower to start a habit and the least to continue it. Here's a step by step manner to start a habit:

1. Decide the habit you want to create.
2. Maintain a continuous streak with no exceptions.

The time you need to maintain the streak varies. Some say 100 days, some say 21 days, some even say you form a habit the moment you decide to create a habit, but it really doesn't matter. Maintain your continuous streak until you feel pulled towards the task, until it takes considerable willpower not to do the same.

- We are what we repeatedly do. Excellence then, is not an act, but a habit.
- Aristotle

And there you are! You have a fresh new habit. This can probably be expanded to fit a whole book, but this is all that you have to do. I hope this will help you in every field of your life. Now, let's move onto our real topic...

Here is an Android App suggestion that can help you track your habits: Loop - Habit Tracker by Alison S Xavier.

How does it apply to time management?

I promised you in the previous chapter that the time management system (TMS) will take care of your time without you having to think about it, and this is how I plan to do it – make the TMS your habit. Make it a part of your life. Embed it so deep within you that you need not concentrate on managing your time; the system does all the work for you. This is how successful people manage their time. They have made productivity and efficiency a powerful habit, so they find it frustrating or unnatural to remain sloppy and inefficient. Once you get a system in place, there's no turning back. You will rest assured that your work is done on time, and you have peace of mind for life, not for your work alone, but for life!

The Investment Mentality

You are given $100 to survive for an entire month. In such a situation, how would you use your $100? You would know every penny that gets spent; you will make sure every penny is spent towards meeting your necessities. You will constantly feel the crunch of money and will count of every loss. Many do not realize it is the same deal with time. Everyday life gives you a bucket of minutes, which you can use to build your empire or to empty it down the drain. It is you who should decide what you will do with it.

-Time is non-refundable, use it with intention.
-Unknown

Life is conservative and gives you only a generous 1440 minutes a day, which is nowhere sufficient to meet the current requirements. Work has increased drastically, but the amount of time has remained constant. While you cannot ask for more time, what you can do is use every minute of the day judicially, just like you would do in a scenario of a money crunch. Be "aware" of every minute of your day; make sure that not a minute of your day gets wasted. To do this, develop the investment mentality. An investment mentality is a change in mindset that makes sure you exploit every minute of your day to the maximum. Once you are aware of every minute that makes up your day, start "investing" them into your various obligations. "Invest" time in work, "invest" time in family, "invest" time in your body. Even if you are sitting idle, make sure you are "investing" your time to sit idle. Be allergic to wastage and smart on the activities you put your time into! Remember one simple thing - each minute wasted is time you won't get back. This small shift in mindset can take you a great distance.

Now that you know the investment mentality, the challenge is to apply it in your life. The biggest problem you would face is keeping the investment mentality in your mind when flooded with work and responsibilities. You become so preoccupied in work you wouldn't even think of this concept. That is where a "focus grabber" comes into the picture. I just made up that name, so call it what you wish. A focus grabber is any item in your immediate surrounding that can remind you to invest time well. I wear a bracelet or band around my wrist to remind me. Every time I see the bracelet, I say to myself "I should use my time well." It works as a constant reminder and as a source of positive affirmations. You could try something helpful for you; you could change your computer or phone wallpaper to: invest time. You could print it out on a paper and stick it on your work desk. Be creative with it!

Which focus grabber do you think is the most effective?

Click here and help fellow readers find their focus grabbers through the Facebook group

Or go to http://bit.ly/TMSgroup

Feel Amazing All the Time!

Have you ever felt so productive that you could move mountains? Have you ever been able to complete a lot of work in very little time? Have you ever felt an unstoppable surge of energy where you finished all your work before time? It could be the other way around, too, when you simply cannot get past one page of your project no matter what you do, when you are just too tired or sleepy to complete your work. This is precisely what your "state of mind" does to you. Your state is an emotional condition that can affect your productivity in a positive or negative way. To put it in a daily context, it is our "mood" to work or not to work. Have you ever said – "I don't feel like working now, I am not in a mood"? Now that's your state speaking!

Wouldn't all your work be complete if you could access your productive state at will? That is how productive people get a lot done in very little time. While most of us have access to our productive state at times, it is when you can call your productive state at will that you can get the most done in less time. So, the question remains, how can you access your productive state at will? Is it even possible? The answer is yes! You can feel the way you want at any given time. That is the secret of the successful. But how?

You can access your state in two ways - your psychology and your physiology. Take care of your mind and body, and you will have a productive day. It's that simple! Being in a "bad mood" is a choice, and you can alter it easily.

First, let's learn how you can control your psychology to be at an optimum state all the time.

Your psychology

Passion towards your work is the first step towards a good psychology. It is the most important element of a successful person. It does not matter if you are a janitor, a stay at home parent, or a CEO of a multinational company; if you absolutely love your work, nothing can stop you from growing. Love the work you do. But the question remains - how do you love something you absolutely don't?

> *- The only way to do great work is to love what you do.*
> *- Steve Jobs*

You can do this by changing your "perspective" on tasks and things. Everything you know about your world is what you "perceive" about the world, not the reality. I will repeat that for you - your world in your mind is simply a perception of the real world. It is what you think about the world, not the real world. To give you a simple example, I hate seafood! I just can't stand the smell of it. Does that make seafood bad? No! That's my view of it; there are lots of people out there who absolutely adore seafood. You see the world through a pair of lenses, and the quality of the lenses determines the quality of your world. It's easy to switch out the lenses to make your life better and to look at things from a different angle. And how do you change the lenses to your mind? - By languaging your thoughts well.

Before we discuss more on that, let me ask you a casual question. Do you love potato chips? Especially when they have been freshly prepared! Hot, crispy, delicate chips that just melt into your mouth as you bite into it. It would be heavenly, wouldn't it? But what if I told you the same chips were prepared in stale, black colored oil, with no heed to hygiene, and the potatoes used for it were 2 months old and rotten. Would you still love them?

It's that easy to change your perspective on things! Language your thoughts differently and concentrate on what matters to you. Find the positives of your work and concentrate on them; don't let the negatives rule your mind. Every work has its positives and negatives. If you feel your work is all negative, with no benefit, why are you working on it in the first place?

The same way, cleaning dishes, taking out the garbage, arranging those messed up papers, working with that uncooperative client, learning that one horrid chapter for the test etc. are not bad. You perceive it as bad. Train your mind to look at them with positivity, and you will find they don't stay on your "pending tasks" list for long.

Language your work differently and you can look at your work differently. Call your business tasks "my path to add value to millions of people." Call cleaning the dishes as "turning dirt into sparkling white dishes." Find creative ways to name it. And don't worry! It's all in your mind; no one's going to know you call your documents "Bobby." Be creative with it and most importantly - have fun!

-Work because you want to, not because you have to.
-Soorej Gopi

A morning routine is also an excellent way to keep your mind in a good state. What you do immediately after you wake up decides how your state will be the whole day. Spend your morning hours in peace and happiness, and you are assured to be in an amazing state the whole day. I have a whole chapter on morning ritual later in this book. So, I don't want to give away everything about morning rituals just yet. We will get to it eventually.

Your physiology

- Motion creates emotion!

- Anthony Robbins

If you ever feel you are being unproductive, there's a good chance you have been sitting with little activity for some time. Your body is built to be active and constantly moving. When you defy the rules of your body, your body rebels and stops listening to your mind. Give your body what it needs, and it will forever cooperate with you.

The second step to maintaining a good state is having an active and healthy body. An unhealthy body can never house a healthy mind; it will only breed laziness. Be active, move around, work out, eat healthy, and keep your blood pumping! You need to be physically fit and active to be at your best state. A new reason to be healthy, eh?

The Two-Minute Fix

I have a powerful tool to feel good at any time in just 2 minutes! The next time you feel lazy and unproductive -

1) Turn on your favorite song

2) Drink 2 big glasses of water

3) Get on your feet and do a few jumping jacks for a minute

4) Close your eyes, breathe deep and slow for another minute

And there you are! All fixed and good to go! I don't want to ruin the crispness by explaining how it works, but it surely works! You can feel the stress as it leaves your head to put you in a productive mood instantly. Don't believe me? Why don't you try it right now? I'll wait….

It's natural to sulk and stay on the couch when you are not in a good mood or in bad state, but I want you to challenge your natural instincts. Be the most active when you are lazy; workout the hardest when you are sad; be the most productive when you have no motivation to work. Maintain this until you have created a habit of being in your best state at all times.

Book Suggestion: Unlimited power – Anthony Robbins.

TMS ingredient in this chapter:

1. *Make the TMS an everlasting habit.*

2. *Conserve every minute of your day with the investment mentality.*

3. *Be in a good state at all times by keeping your mind and body in top condition.*

4. *Practice the two-minute fix every time you feel low.*

Chapter 3

Declutter: Clean Up Your Stream

It's All Simple

What is 12+57+89+78+14?

Did you find the solution? Or did you just continue reading?
You continued reading, didn't you?

What is 100+100+50?

Yeah, now you did the math!

Both questions have the same answer (I had a calculator). When both problems had the same outcome, why did you solve the second problem and not the first one?

The first problem is complex, and it requires a degree of effort for the brain to comprehend (if you are someone like me, you would require a great degree of effort). Even if you didn't have to solve the problem, a simple glance at the problem can give you a heavy feeling in your gut. Did you feel it? Why don't you try it? Give the first equation another read (you don't have to solve it) .... Did you feel it now?

The second equation requires no effort to solve. You probably would find it hard NOT to think of the answer while you read it. Give the second equation another try. Can you finish the sentence without thinking of 250?

When things around you are simple and organized, your brain finds patterns to recognize them and does not take up any mental juice to identify and process them. That's exactly what happens in this example. Your brain needs considerable processing power to solve the first problem, while it can solve the second problem using familiar patterns it has created over the years. To quote another example of this phenomenon, I am sure all of you have experienced the "settling-in" experience of a new house or workplace. The first few days are always confusing and unnatural. It requires some "getting used to" before you feel at ease in your new environment. This is because your brain is still in the process of making patterns of things around you. When your brain is finished with this process, you feel cozy and at home in your new workplace or house.

When a messy mathematical equation can make you feel disheartened, try assessing the damage you can do to your brain when you work in a cluttered and unorganized environment. Your brain has so many more items to process and will find it so much more difficult to make familiar patterns. Unnecessary things compete for your brain's attention, which reduces its attention span and increases stress. Keep your environment simple and organized, and your brain will easily create familiar patterns to reduce its processing work. You can concentrate better on things that matter and come up with solutions easier. So, let's get decluttering - one field at a time!

- Simplicity is the ultimate sophistication
- Leonardo DaVinci

Declutter Your Environment

Decluttering my workplace is the first thing I do before I work on any project. I make sure my workplace has only the necessary items and nothing extra - not even an item of decoration. My workplace might not be the fanciest, but I can say it is one of the most efficient ones I know. An organized workplace gives you a feeling of accomplishment and pride. The feeling of happiness and pride you get once you have organized your surroundings is indescribable. An unorganized work area is a source of negative vibes. It constantly reminds you of your pending work and lack of organizational skills. Some of us are so used to living in an unorganized way we have made it our primary state. We do not feel a need to change and continue living an unorganized life without needing to change.

- Organizing is what you do before you do something, so that when you do it, it is not all mixed up.
- A.A.Milne

Here's how you can declutter your surroundings/workplace:

1. **Less Stuff:** More things = More clutter. Want to clear up your surroundings? - Get rid of things you do not need. For the purpose of my topic, it would be sufficient if you store it in a place you can't see it, but it really is not the best technique to get organized. If you work in an office environment, have only the necessary files and papers on your table; keep the rest in your drawer until you need it. Simply make sure the only things in sight are the things you are working on. Anything else is plain clutter!

    - The most important things in life aren't things
    - Anthony J. D'Angelo

2. **Have specific places for specific items:** When you have fewer items, it is easy to assign specific spots for every item. If an item is not in its spot, put it in its place immediately.

    - A place for everything, everything in its place.
    - Benjamin Franklin

3. **Don't create a mess:** The best way to stay uncluttered - don't create the clutter in the first place. Keep things well-organized in places they belong. A small change in your routine activity can save you from clutter. (We will discuss more on this topic in chapter #7 – <u>Manage Time Like the Corporates: Streamline Your Stream.</u>)

4. **Periodic reviews:** Make it a habit to check on your things periodically. Make sure you have no unnecessary items and all things are in the places where they belong.

Book suggestion: The Life-Changing Magic of Tidying up by Marie Kondo.

Declutter Your Digital Life

Decluttering your physical environment is an age-old technique, but what about the virtual worlds we live in? New technology has provided us the opportunity to have fresh varieties of clutter. Unnecessary files, videos, photos, and all kinds of apps for purposes the developer alone knows! Decluttering your devices is of special importance if you work primarily on a computer. For example, this entire book was typed on a 12-year-old desktop running windows XP - one of those computers with the small screened HUGE monitor that likes to go red every now and then, coupled with a noisy CPU cooling fan and a floppy drive. The only thing it could handle was my minimalistic typing application and a web browser to access Google docs. This was my way to stay undisturbed and decluttered while I work on the book. I don't advise you to do the same, but you get the idea!

Here are methods by which you can keep your digital life clutter free:

1. **Uninstall unnecessary apps:** Keep your phone and computer minimal. Unnecessary applications cause clutter, distract you with random notifications, and can be a source of distraction. Uninstall the apps you feel you will need some time in the future. You really do not need it on your computer or phone; you can simply download it when you need it. Keep your desktop or app drawer minimal.

2. **Master your mails:** Unsubscribe from all unnecessary promotional mail you receive to make room for important mail. Archive the unnecessary mail and categorize the mail you wish to keep. Make separate lists for mail of different subjects. I have a list for all the invoices of devices I own, a list for all my work-related mail, a list to keep the important legal documents, a list to keep the important items I have mailed to myself. The mail you move to lists will not appear in your primary inbox. This alone can clear up a lot of mail from your inbox.

3. **Take advantage of cloud:** The ability to store a large number of files on the internet gives you an opportunity to clear up your devices. A cloud storage can be an attic for your digital files, where it will remain accessible and safe until you need it.

4. **Organize your files:** Organize your files into various folders and subfolders. Do not leave them lying on your home screen. If you can find any file you need without searching around, you have satisfied this step.

5. **Detach from it:** All of us like to live a fast digital life, but taking time off from your devices can be very relaxing! While avoiding it is not an option, some time off regularly can elevate your mood and leave you feeling happy.

Declutter Your Mind

A cluttered environment is bad, but a cluttered mind is worse. That's right; your mind can get cluttered too! You may work all day and have a well-organized environment, but the reflection will never be pretty if the water is not still. Keeping your mind clutter free is equally important if not more important. But what makes up the clutter in your mind? Allow me to explain using an example:

Similar to our brain, a CPU chip on the motherboard does the processing activities in a computer. If you look closely into the functioning of a CPU, you will notice the CPU does not store the data it processes. Its sole objective is to process data and provide output. The data that must be processed is stored in a temporary location, called RAM, from where the CPU can easily retrieve it. The CPU is meant only for data processing and not for storage. The same goes with the processing units of a human body. The brain accepts problems and provides solutions for it. It is a processing device and is designed to find solutions, not hold our problems. Unfortunately, that is exactly what most of us make our brains do.

Your things to remember, pending appointments, personal problems, work to do etc. form the clutter in your mind. Our brains are not designed to store all these issues; you give it a problem, and it will come up with solutions. Your brain doesn't care about your meetings and problems; give it an input and it will give you an output. It's that simple! But all of us make our brains do the exact thing it was not designed to do! We clog it and leave it so messed up it has no room to do the things expected of it. What happens when you make a machine do something it is not designed to do? It heats up! Now, you know why and how you get stressed!

If at any time you feel you are being stressed out – take it as a reminder for you to declutter your mind. Clear the clutter in your brain, and you will unlock its true potential. It is fresh and ready to tackle any work thrown at it. With a fresh mind and brain, your work time will reduce and productivity will soar. But what can we do to declutter our minds?

Think on paper! A piece of paper - the RAM for your mind. All your appointments, schedules, and to-dos should be written on paper. This is why most great people advise to create a habit of writing regularly. The paper, not your brain, carries the weight of your problems. Allow the brain to do what it was designed to do. Write down all your problems in a detailed manner and think of a solution by analyzing the writings. This alone can help you boost your skills in problem solving. No matter the problem, pour out all your emotions, thoughts, and ideas onto a piece of paper and try to find a solution by analyzing and working with the sheet, rather than in your mind. Your brain loses a ton of weight once you write everything down; with its newfound vigor and freedom, your brain may run the great distance to give you the perfect solution you seek. You will instantly notice a drop in your stress level. We will learn more about decluttering your mind by using a powerful tool in chapter #6 - <u>Scheduling: Plan Your Stream</u>.

> *- Reduce the noise in your life to be able hear what really matters.*
> *- Soorej Gopi*

App Suggestion: Evernote is a writing app that can help you with your writing habit.

TMS ingredients in this chapter:

1. *Be organized as it can save you a lot of mental juice.*
2. *Keep your surroundings, workplace, and mind free from clutter.*

Chapter 4

Proper Prioritization: Direct Your Stream

"I Am Going to The Himalayas"

It was just another day in my busy schedule. I was working "hard", very hard! I watched a motivational video, but it did not help. I also took a break, a nap, a snack, a talk, and a walk, but I just couldn't work! I would have jumped off a cliff if I was asked to, but not work for another second. I just couldn't do it anymore! And my work? – miles from completion! I wanted to throw all my work and go to the Himalayas to become a hermit. A peaceful mind was the only thing I needed at that moment.

Have you ever had such an experience? Or even worse – do you live your everyday life this way? Have you ever been so fed up with your work you wanted to pull your hair out? The most probable answer is – yes. That could have been the very reason you picked up this book. Life can get hard. Through this chapter, I want to help you reduce, if not completely stop, this absurd feeling of helplessness.

Don't Work Hard!

From our first memories of life, we have been taught to work hard. "Anything worthwhile requires hard work" is what we believe and work towards. But what if I told you things need not be that way. Things need not be hard all the time. You need to work "just enough" on the "right things" to succeed. If hard work was the judging factor for success, the people who carry heavy loads on their heads to earn their daily bread would have been the most successful. Fortunately, that's not how the world works.

Certain tasks can be daunting initially; it might require extra effort from your side. But as time passes, your body finds a rhythm as you continue doing the task regularly. If you cannot find a rhythm in your work, you are pushing yourself too hard. Although growth comes only when you push yourself, you cannot work hard forever; you will drain out and lose motivation and willpower to continue working. It won't be long before you would want to go to the Himalayas. Successful people do not necessarily work "harder" than the rest, but they work enough on the right things to be on top of the game. Don't work hard – work smart!

- Working hard and working smart sometimes can be two different things.
- Byron Dorgan.

There is a fine line between working hard and working smart. When you try to give your energy to all the work on your list, you are working hard. When you "prioritize" and work on the necessary tasks, you are working smart. Like we discussed previously, our tasks have increased immensely while our time has remained the same. It does not require rocket science to figure out that, when the amount of work is more than the time at hand, some work will definitely be left out. Decide which tasks are worth your time and which tasks can be done some other time. Accept that your work can never be "completely complete" but promise to do your best.

My solution to this problem – prioritization. Honestly, I was not a believer of prioritization. I always had the notion that all work is equally important and all of them need to be attended on time. While my belief allowed me to work in an excellent manner, it wasn't long before it broke me from the inside. I was leading a miserable life. I had lost connections with my loved ones, my weight increased drastically, and I had lost the essence of life. But how can you decide which tasks to skip and which ones to work on immediately? Let's discuss...

- Slow down and enjoy life. It's not only the scenery you miss by going too fast – you also miss the sense of where you are going and why.
- Eddie Cantor

Pareto's 80/20 Rule

Have you ever taken time to notice how fascinating a tree is? Think about it, a humongous thousand-ton tree grows from a tiny seed. The small task of putting a seed in the ground and watering it has the result of creating something that will last decades and provide fruits your entire life. The effort needed to build something so colossal is so minimal. The same applies to our lives. We need not put in tons of effort to get results; take the right seed and put in enough efforts to make it grow. Your efforts will give you multiplied results. The only challenge is selecting the right seed. That's where the 80/20 rule comes in - it helps you choose the right seed.

Vilfredo Pareto was an Italian economist, who found a rather odd ratio in the inputs and outputs of a task. He found 20% of the peapods in his garden produced 80% of the peas. He also found the ratio in the land ownership patterns of Italy - 20% of the people held 80% of the land. This ratio has since been termed as "Pareto's 80/20 rule." It wasn't long before people found the applicability of this ratio in many other fields.

20% clients provide 80% of the sales revenue.

20% of the people in a team produce 80% of the results.

20% of a portfolio creates 80% of the income.

20% of your emails contain 80% of the information you need.

20% of the items on your Facebook wall catch 80% of your attention.

20% of the number of items on your computer takes up 80% of its space.

The list goes on and on, but on the same simple principle - "20% efforts = 80% results." Concentrate your efforts on the right 20%, and 80% of your work is done. This is the best possible way to prioritize your tasks. It is up to you to find your 20% of work. Writing this book was only 20% of the work I had to do each day, but it provided me with most satisfaction, even if I had skipped my other tasks. Following a healthy sleep schedule makes up only 20% of the things I do to maintain energy, but it provides me with the most energy to sustain my day.

- Most of us spend too much time on what is urgent and not enough time on what is important.

- Stephen R.Covey

The idea here is to find out your most important tasks. It could be anything - concentrating on the employees of your company, giving extra focus to those important clients, concentrating on those important chapters to score the most marks, taking care of your children etc. I would suggest you pause reading and take a minute to identify the most important tasks of your day. The 20% of your tasks that can give you maximum results and satisfaction.

Done? I hope you could successfully identify your important tasks. Now, let's discuss what we should do with them....

What's your most important 20% task each day?

Click here to share it with the community on Facebook

Or go to http://bit.ly/TMSgroup

Concentrated Efforts

Let's bring back old Ralph for another story. Now that his cabin is long gone, he decides to dig a well. He set out early that morning, finds a good spot, and starts digging. Being the impatient man he is, he hoped to finish his work fast and return home early with the sweet taste of fresh water on his tongue. He dug away for hours without a break, waiting for the moment his spade digs in through a rich vein of water. Old Ralph dug for a few hours and sank in 15 cubits deep before he got too tired to dig another second. Exhausted, he threw himself under the shade of the tree beside the road as he watched busy strangers hustling to work. Noticing the tired old man, a friendly stranger stopped for a minute to ask if everything was all right.

"How are you doing, my good man? Why do you look so miserable on such a lovely spring day?" asked the intrigued face.

"You won't believe my luck. I just dug 15 cubits at that spot with no sign of water!" responded Ralph pointing at the spot.

"Well, today is your day, old man! Thank your darn good luck I stopped by. It was only a month back I had a well dug, and I struck water in just 15 minutes of digging! Would you believe that? Come with me. I will show you the spot."

Desperate to complete his work fast, Ralph follows the stranger to a new spot and digs with all his might. He dug another 20 cubits but with no sign of water.

"15 minutes he said? Huh! It's been almost an hour of digging! Where's all the water?" Ralph screamed.

Intrigued by the voice coming from the pit, the town scholar peeped in to find angry Ralph covered in mud.

"Bless the heavenly stars! What are you doing, Ralph? Don't dig a well here! Don't you know the ground is covered with rocks in this area? Why didn't you ask for my advice before you started your work?"

Boiling with anger, Ralph found a new spot for his well and started all over for the third time! He decided this would be his last attempt at the well! A few hours went by, and he sank another 20 cubits in the new spot with his gushing sweat being the only sign of water. Ralph cursed his luck and every other person he knew! The sun had set, and it was getting dark. Ralph called it a day and went home to tell his story to his wife.

She was awe-struck hearing Ralph's story!

"55 cubits? You dug 55 cubits?" she exclaimed.

"What were you thinking, Ralph? You could've gone right through the rocky surface of the village to strike water in any area of the town if you had dug 55 cubits at one spot!"

"I know that!" Ralph snapped back, too proud to hurt his ego.....

> *- Effort is important but knowing where to make an effort makes all the*
> *difference*
> *- Unknown*

You might think Ralph was stupid to dig holes all over town. But don't you think this is how we work, too? We give our attention to everything that might arise in a day and end up with nothing in hand. Don't be another well digger! Concentrate your efforts on your most important tasks and leave the rest. Do not drown in the endless river of small tasks. They keep popping up, and you can never be done with them.

Now that you have found your most important tasks using the 80/20 principle, allocate the biggest chunk of your time to that task. Do it to maximum satisfaction before you come back to the numerous other tasks. As for your other tasks, you could try one of the below:

1. **Outsource:** Try to outsource or assign some other person to do mindless tasks for you. Do not do everything on your own. Your time and willpower is more valuable than the hire charges.

2. **Procrastinate:** Yes, I am asking you to procrastinate. Anything used well can be helpful. Procrastinate your 80% of tasks to make time for the important 20%. Forget about them until it's absolutely necessary to complete them. This is "selective procrastination."

3. **Defer it:** Do the smaller tasks when tired or out of willpower. I do my smaller tasks in the evening when I have no willpower left. This way, I finish my small tasks without it taking a toll on my willpower.

4. **Skip it:** Learning to skip tasks is an important part of a good TMS. Small tasks keep coming up, and it is our instinct to finish them fast to do other tasks. This gives us a dopamine rush, which gives us an illusion of satisfaction when all our "real" work is pending. Ask yourself this question: "Do I really need to do this? Does it have any major consequences if left undone?" If the answer is a no, skip that task all together.

- Deciding what not to do is as important as deciding what to do.

- Steve Jobs

Once you clear out all the small tasks, you will notice you have little to do. This simple method of prioritizing can save you a ton of time and ensure you do not end up in the Himalayas.

So, what is the best time of day to do your most important task? We will learn that in the next chapter......

TMS ingredients in this chapter:
1. *Don't work hard! Work smart by prioritizing your tasks.*
2. *Apply the Pareto's principle as a method of prioritizing. Use it to find your most important 20% tasks.*
3. *Concentrate your efforts on your most important tasks and let your other tasks take a step back.*
4. *Apply various techniques to detach from the remaining 80% tasks.*

Chapter 5

Master Your Mornings: Empower Your Stream

-The sun has not caught me in bed in fifty years.

-Thomas Jefferson

What do you do after you wake up? If you are like most people, you stay in bed until the last minute, break the snooze button until the alarm doesn't want to ring anymore, and when you are finally out of bed, you are irritated, groggy, and stressed. You are immediately reminded of the work you have to get done that day, and with your half open eyes, you pick up your phone to check the notifications. Probably, you are late, so you curse your sleep, freshen up, and head for work as quickly as you can. Not quite a good start to a day of unlimited possibilities and opportunities, don't you think? Let's see what others do immediately after they wake up...

Barack Obama starts his day 2 hours before any event. He works out for 45 minutes a day and has his breakfast. He says: "The rest of my time will be more productive if you give me my workout time."

Steve Jobs, in his speech to the graduating class of Stanford University, told "For the past 33 years, I have looked in the mirror every morning and asked myself - 'if today were the last day of my life, would I want to do what I am about to do today?' Whenever the answer has been no for too many days in a row, I know I need to change something."

Bill Gates spends an hour on the treadmill, while watching courses from the Teaching Company.

Howard Schultz says: "I get up at 4:30am every morning to walk my three dogs and work out."

Benjamin Franklin would get up at 5am every day and ask himself: "What good shall I do today?"

Oprah Winfrey does 20 minutes of meditation to clear her mind and she has this to say about her morning ritual: "I walked away feeling fuller than when I'd come in. Full of hope, a sense of contentment, and deep joy. Knowing for sure that even in the daily craziness that bombards us from every direction, there is still the constancy of stillness. Only from that space can you create your best work and your best life."

Deepak Chopra says: "I, of course, meditate for two hours every morning. It's part of my schedule; I wake up at 4am every day and I love it."

The list is endless. All of them have the same quality - they wake up early and spend quality time with themselves before tackling their outside world. After all, you are the most important thing you have. You deserve to be pampered and treated well.

We discussed in the first chapter that our day is a stream. What decides the size of a stream? - Its source. The place where a river originates decides the size and power of a stream. The same way, the power of your day is decided by its origin - the morning hours. Through this chapter, we will turn your stream into a mighty river crushing every task in its path. I want you to create a habit of waking up early and spending time with yourself before starting your day. It is an important part of your TMS. In a broad sense, there are two ways to ensure you have an amazing start to your day. Either you can do a morning ritual or you can eat a live frog.....

- A day well begun is a day well done
- Soorej Gopi

A Morning Ritual

There are many successful people out there who give credit of all their success to one simple habit – a habit they did regularly to become successful, a habit they continue doing regularly to remain successful. There are many books and courses praising the same habit, yet lots of people are unaware of such a golden habit.

The highly successful people start their day on an amazing note. As we just saw, they know the power and benefit of the morning hours. We too can do the same by making the morning ritual a solid part of our TMS. There's no better way to start your day. A morning ritual helps you be proactive and actively control your day to make sure it goes the way you want it to. It also cultivates good emotions in you to help you start the day with all the motivation in the world!

- Either you run the day or the day runs you

- Jim Rohn

Here are a few activities you can do to make sure you start your day on the right foot.

1. **Drink water:** Once you are out of bed, freshen up and drink two huge glasses of water. After a long night's sleep, your body is dehydrated and craves water. If you feel tired immediately after you get out of bed, your body probably is dehydrated. Lack of water, not lack of sleep, is the reason for this common problem.

2. **Get pumping:** Your body has been with little movement for almost seven to eight hours. You need to wake up your body from within to get rid of the sleep inertia and grogginess. Do a few stretches or jumping jacks to get your blood pumping and mind running. This will also make sure you don't go back to bed.

3. **Meditate:** There are countless books, blogs, and research that praise the benefits of meditation. I am sure all of you have tried meditation at least once in your life, but just wasn't able to keep up with it for more than a few days. That's where the

morning ritual can help you. When it is a part of your morning ritual, you are compelled to do it to complete your morning ritual on time.

4. **Cultivate emotions:** Repairing and revitalizing your mind is as important as healing your body. You mind too would have probably taken a beating from yesterday's stress and day of intense work. It needs time to rejuvenate and get to where it needs to be. This is why you need to cultivate emotions first thing in the morning. Close your eyes and be grateful for everything in life. It need not be anything big; be thankful for having a roof over your head, be thankful for the food you had the previous day, be thankful you have a pair of good eyes, be thankful for every small thing in life. You will realize how blessed you are when you stop to notice all the things God has blessed you with.

5. **Plan your day:** This is the part where you are proactive. The morning time is the best time to plan your day. Take a piece of paper and write down all the things you will achieve that day. You now know what exactly is expected from you that day and can put down each of them. (We will learn the Planning process in the next chapter Scheduling: Plan Your Stream.)

6. **Read:** When I was still in school, my teachers used to say that things learnt in the morning are things you will never forget. I remember none of those poems I learnt in school, but I believe morning time is the best time to learn anything new. With a fresh mind, you will have doubled the normal attention span.

7. **Exercise:** Make exercise a part of your morning ritual, and you won't have to allocate time for it. Your body gets what it wants first thing in the morning and will reward you handsomely with a productive and active day.

As I am tied down to my topic of discussion, I am limited on the information I can give you on this topic. Hence, I would like to suggest a video that goes into the details of all the above steps.

Click here or go to https://www.youtube.com/watch?v=PliFBr__T7Y .

Eat a Frog

How would it be never to have a bad day again? Wouldn't it be amazing to finish the most important task of your day, even before the world is awake? That's exactly what Mark Twain's advice is! Mark Twain said: *"If it's your job to eat a frog, it's best to do it first thing in the morning. And if it's your job to eat two frogs, it's best to eat the biggest one first."*

The most important task in a day is your frog, as it is the most undesirable and tedious task you have for the day. Finish it first thing in the morning and you would not have to worry about having a bad day. An excellent way to start a day with endless opportunities, don't you think? Once you are done and dusted with the biggest and ugliest task for the day, going through smaller tasks shouldn't be much of a problem. The fire in your gut will burn stronger than a thousand flames and all your work? - Done!

The 120-Minute Superhero

I believe all of us have a superhero inside us. A hero who is creatively and physically superior than the normal you; a hero who can crush any task thrown at him with the least efforts. But he is unpredictable and hard to catch as he does not like to stick around for a long time. He comes immediately after you wake up and leaves exactly 2 hours later, without saying a word. He does not work on our convenience, but we can catch him by exploiting these 2 hours to the maximum.

The first two hours immediately after you wake up are sacred. "Sacred" that's what I call it! Yet, it is the most abused and neglected time of the day. After a long night of rest, your body and mind is ready to tackle anything you throw at it. And it will tackle it in such a way you never knew you could. What better time to eat your frog? To illustrate, the bulk of this book was written during these two hours of the day. Almost all anecdotes used here were made during these hours. You can finish your entire day's work in just these two hours if you put your mind to it. A person who dares to waste this time does not know the value of it.

-Lose an hour in the morning and you'll be looking for it all day.
-Richard Whately.

What's Stopping You?

I am sure this is not the first time you are hearing this advice. From Benjamin Franklin's famous quote "early to bed, early to rise makes a man healthy, wealthy and wise" to your parents asking you to go to bed early when you were still a kid, the advice is something you've known for years. Yet, few follow it. Why is that?

This is the main problem I would like to address here. Giving advice is easy, putting it into practice? - Not so easy. Let's tackle that with an incident that happened a few days back. I was having a chat with my friend Roger on the same topic. He firmly stood by his point that he is a night owl and has achieved great things at night, rather than in the morning hours. He even told me he tried waking up early for a few days, but it just wasn't for him, and it left him tired and irritated the whole day. I am sure many of you agree and are on the same path as Roger. Instead of sparking an argument with him, I asked him to give the advice one last try, but this time, stick to it and maintain a streak for 30 days. Being the gentleman he is, Roger agreed and said he would get back to me with results. Roger had this to say:

"I was very skeptical about giving this another try, but I gave it one last shot. The first few days were painful! I couldn't fall asleep at such an early hour. I couldn't get out of bed without having to snooze at least 3 times. There were days when I went back to bed immediately after waking up, but I kept at it in spite of all that. By the second week, I started to gain momentum - it was much easier to fall asleep and wake up now. By the third week, I no longer needed the alarm. I was wide awake at 5am and at my best within a few minutes of getting out of bed. It was only then that I started to feel the differences. Waking up early gave me a head start to the day, and I remained at my best the rest of the day. Even though I was a night person, working in the mornings has very different kinds of advantages. More people should try implementing it."

Why did it work for Roger this time, when it didn't when he tried it previously? - Roger made waking up early a habit! He stuck to it long enough for it to become a habit. He embedded it deep within him until he could exploit it to its maximum. This gave time for his body clock to adjust according to the new timings. This is where most people go wrong - they don't try it long enough for it to become a habit. It is easy to stay awake at night as you have many distractions and things you could do, but it is different with the morning hours. Now that you know the reasons and method, why don't you try it? If Roger and I could do it, you surely can do it too. You know what you have to do; insert it into your TMS and make it a lifelong habit.

> *-The first step to win yourself is to wake up early.*
> *-Sukant Ratnakar.*

What time did you wake up today? Having trouble waking up early?
Click here and let's help each other out through Facebook
Or go to http://bit.ly/TMSgroup

TMS ingredients in this chapter:

1. *Wake up early and change the way you use your morning time.*

2. *Do a morning ritual to be in a good state of mind every day.*

3. *Work on your most important tasks first thing in the morning.*

4. *Harness the power of your superhero and exploit the first 120 minutes of each day.*

Chapter 6

Scheduling: Plan Your Stream

"Anything worthwhile requires time and effort." Take a second to read that quote again. I am sure all of you agree with it. Through this chapter, I will make sure that quote sinks deep into your TMS and becomes a way of life for you to follow throughout your life. We will build our system of scheduling using this principle. Just like a plant that must be watered daily, the tasks in your life need constant attention and time for it to bear fruit. If left unattended, the plant will dry out and weeds or smaller trivial tasks will take its place. Important things must be given its time, they need to be nurtured, they need to be taken care of, and the weeds must be kept out! For instance, how do you plan to achieve your dream body if you don't consciously work out? How can you have a colorful life if you do not spend time with your loved ones? How will your work ever be complete if you do not give it enough time?

-Spend time doing things that matter

-Robin Sharma

The not so secret method to control your day and end up satisfied with your work is to allot time for each of your important tasks. Give each task the time it needs, and it will give you results you seek. Make sure the trivial tasks of your day don't disrupt the time you allot for your important tasks. But the problem is that most of us let our streams find its own path; we have no control over the path it takes. It flows according to the slope of the land, the bumps on the way, and the turns in the rocks. Our schedule gets affected by everything the day throws at us, and we react to the things that show up throughout the day, rather than working on our most important tasks. Through this chapter, we will put a rein over our stream and make it flow the way we want it and to the place we want it, without being affected by the bumps and slopes of our day.

The method we will learn in this chapter is almost 250 years old! Allow me to show you the schedule of one the founding fathers of the United States of America. Yes, Benjamin Franklin used this technique as far back as the 1770's.

How Benjamin Franklin Made His Schedule

Given below is an image of Benjamin's Franklin's schedule taken from his autobiography originally published in 1791.

The morning question, What good shall I do this day?	5	Rise, wash, and address *Powerful Goodness*; contrive day's business and take the resolution of the day; prosecute the present study; and breakfast.
	6	
	7	
	8	
	9	Work.
	10	
	11	
	12	Read or overlook my accounts, and dine.
	1	
	2	
	3	Work.
	4	
	5	
	6	Put things in their places, supper, music, or diversion, or conversation; examination of the day.
	7	
	8	
	9	
Evening question, What good have I done today?	10	
	11	
	12	
	1	Sleep.
	2	
	3	
	4	

Quite minimalistic, don't you think? Here, we see an excellent example of time blocking. Simple and practical! It's not often you see successful people walking around with huge diaries containing complex schedules and tables. They don't apply complex formulas to decide what they have to do in a day. They have time blocks! If you spend all your willpower deciding what to do, when are you going to work on it? Hence, it is only logical to keep your planning phase as minimalistic as possible to conserve your willpower as much as possible.

What is a Time Block?

You have been invited for a talk with the CEO of a huge tech company or with one of your favorite singers. But you are too busy and have countless tasks to do. Would you tell him or her you are busy? No! Don't do that! You would push out all your trivial tasks and block time in your calendar for the meeting. Why don't we do the same with our everyday important tasks? After all, they are as important to your life as meeting your favorite celebrity.

That's what a time block is - it literally means the time you have blocked for some activity in your schedule; it is a chunk of your day solely dedicated to one activity. You need to make it a point to allot time for the important 20% of your tasks every day. Fix time for them and follow it no matter how you feel or what you have to do. For instance, are you always running short of time to work on your dream body? A time block is the solution - fix 6am to 7am every morning solely for exercising and let nothing come up during that hour of your day. All your tasks are non-existent at that hour of the day. You have blocked it exclusively for exercising and you will have to do it every day without fail. Consciously recognizing and working on your important tasks make people successful. Your other 80% of the tasks should take a step back to allow room for the important tasks. That's how successful people work; that's how you should work!

Ideally, you should have 4 - 5 time blocks each day. This makes sure the system retains its meaning and is kept as minimalistic as possible. You could have up to a maximum of 7 or 8 time blocks; add more than that and the system loses its meaning. You will be back where you began. To give you a better idea, I will share my own time blocks:

5 am - 9 am	Morning Ritual and Book work.
10 am - 6 pm	Office
7 pm – 7:30 pm	Guitar
8 pm - 10 pm	Family time

How many things do you have to do each day? I have only 4! I am sure all of you can do exceptionally well if you too had only 4 things to do each day. I work my heart out on these items, and that's it! I just had an amazing day! That's all there is to it. The most important tasks of my day are taken care of. What do I have to be stressed about now?

Now that you know what a time block is, why don't you take a piece of paper and fix at least 2 time blocks. Doing it now while it is still fresh in your mind can be beneficial. You need not divide your whole day into time block like Benjamin Franklin did; you can have empty slots where you can catch up on your other tasks or stop to catch your breath.

So, go ahead. I'll wait............

Done? I hope you took action. This book will simply be a rant if you do not take action and apply the principles in your life.

-You delay, but time will not.
-Benjamin Franklin

Your Body Loves a Routine

Have you ever slept at the wrong time of the day and felt sleepy the same time the next day? Or have you ever had your lunch a few hours before your normal lunch time and felt hungry at the same early hour the next day? Or have you stayed up late one night to watch your favorite team play and couldn't get sleep until that late hour the next day? Your body loves predictability and repetition. When you do the same thing at the same time every day, your body adapts to it and becomes comfortable doing the task at that time, which gives a great boost to your efficiency and productivity levels. The same goes with time blocking. Our bodies adapt to a particular work when you do it the same time every day. Or to put it in a simpler way - your body creates a habit. Not only is the method of time blocking simple and practical, but it is also based on the same primary concept of habit creation. Stick to your schedule long enough, and it becomes a part of you. The best part of this method is you will not need to carry around a planning sheet everywhere you go. It's all deep within you, rather than on a sheet of paper you fail to follow. It won't be long before you work on the tasks you assigned for each block without even thinking about them.

The difficult part

When I started this system, I found it challenging as it needed considerable willpower and discipline to follow. It's difficult to switch tasks when you are neck deep in your previous tasks. Your mind does not like to do so. It will force you to remain on the current task. I reached a point where I decided to give up on the system with the thought, "this isn't working for me." Determined to apply it in my life, I thought I would give it one last try, but this time, I would concentrate on just ONE time block. I had a time block for exercising back then, which has become a part of the morning ritual now. Half-heartedly, I gave it shot...

A few days went by and I wasn't having much trouble following the schedule. To my disbelief, I exercised consistently for a whole month! And I hadn't even pushed myself to do it. I felt an urge to exercise every morning. I felt frustrated when I couldn't exercise. I would get out of bed, freshen up, and get on the elliptical trainer with no thought or use of willpower. It was all on autopilot. Amazing! Don't you think? I am sure you could use it too.

So, what went wrong the first time? - I was trying to follow 4 – 5 time blocks at a time! You need an estate full of self-discipline to start 5 time blocks at the same time. You could do it for a day or two, but your body and mind will rebel if it goes more than that. So, don't go too hard on yourself! Take it one at a time. My advice would be to create a solid time block and make it a part of you before you step into another. I know this will take time and probably a few months. But I can promise it will be worth the patience!

Android app suggestion: Timetune by timetune studio

To-do Lists Don't Work?

Now that you have planned the important 20% of the tasks of your day, what happens to the remaining 80%? You can't just ignore them; after all, they make up 80% of all your tasks. Going head-on to tackle them without a plan would be foolish as these 80% tasks are the major reason for stress and confusion among most people. Through this chapter, we will bring clarity to your life by organizing all your countless tasks.

Have you ever been so flooded with work that your mind gives up on you and goes on a break when you absolutely should not be taking a break? Have you been so flooded with work you simply can't figure out what you have to do? I am sure you have. I had such an experience recently. I was going out of town for a week and only had to pack all the clothes, close all my work in the office, submit the report I had completed, assign someone else to continue on my project, apply for leave, buy a few clothes for the trip, book tickets for the travel, book a hotel room, submit a few forms for attestation, talk to the editor of the book, remember to carry all my chargers, decide on dates and means of travel, remember to buy a gift for our host, ask someone to feed the fish at home, blah blah..... Can you imagine tackling all those tasks? Uff! Thinking of it makes me tired. In such a situation, it is impractical to take a calendar and fix time for every task you would have to do. You could finish one of your tasks in the time you take to make a schedule you surely won't keep.

This is where I use the power of "categorizing." I make a categorized to-do list. But that brings us to the famous topic of confusion - "to to-do or not to to-do." Many authors are against the concept of a to-do list and rightly so, as it is more of a wish list than an action list. Tasks can linger in the depths of your to-do list for the entirety of its life. But if used well, a to-do list can be powerful. And how do you do that? We tweak the to-do list, add a few constraints, change its structure, and voila - you have a categorized to-do list.

Coming back to my example of going out of town, this is how I categorised all my work to make a categorized to-do list:

Office work

- Close all my work in office
- Submit the report I had completed
- Apply for leave
- Assign someone else to continue my project

Travel work

- Decide on dates and means of travel

- Buy clothes for the trip
- Pack all the clothes
- Book tickets for the travel
- Book a hotel room
- Buy a gift for our host
- Carry all my chargers

Personal work

- Submit a few forms for attestation
- Talk to the editor of the book
- Ask someone to feed the fish at home

Now, I have just 3 things to do instead of a zillion things to do. Neat eh? Tasks make up a to-do list, but areas or fields make up a categorized to-do list. That is the primary difference. We look at the bigger picture and clear out a lot of tension and confusion. Concentrating on just 3 things will help you do the tasks much faster, and it will clear all the clutter and stress from your mind to give you peace of mind and clarity. This is the power of categorizing! Categorize it the way you want it; for example, I recently categorised my tasks based on time – "today, tomorrow and sometime in the future" or as "urgent and not urgent."

If it can simplify such a complicated situation of going out of town, it can surely work for your everyday tasks. Write down all the tasks you have to do and put it in various categories. That's it – simple and practical!

TMS ingredients in this chapter:

1. *Have control over your day.*
2. *Create time blocks for the important 20% tasks in your day.*
3. *Use a categorized to-do list to tackle the remaining 80% tasks.*

Chapter 7

Manage Time Like the Corporates: Streamline Your Stream

If every employee in a 2000 employee corporate works just a minute extra a day, they can complete the same work that a single employee would take 4 days to complete. A minute of extra work can save a corporate nearly $500 of work! Think about it; it's jaw dropping! When the numbers are so massive, you can only imagine the effort that goes into achieving efficiency and productivity in a place like this. They have intricate procedures and controls to make sure the maximum output is extracted out of each minute a worker puts in. I was fortunate to study a few such methods in the course of my professional studies. Can someone teach you about efficiency better than the corporates?

"Business Process Re-engineering"(BPR)

BPR was a technique developed in the 1990s to help businesses achieve efficiency and reduce their costs. It focused on dramatically increasing the output with reduced costs. It involves redesigning and fundamental rethinking of everything, simply "everything" a corporation does from their fundamental mission statement to their method of working. While all the concepts of BPR cannot be applied to our lives, there are a few fundamental beliefs that can radically increase the time we have in our hands.

BPR states: "most of the processes in an organization might have been developed by the functional units over a period of time without any serious effort to analyze the process or measure their effectiveness." Yeah, I didn't understand that the first time either. Allow me to translate that into English, in the context of time management. Most activities we do regularly are activities we have been doing for a long time. They are activities that have entered our lives through natural learning and years of repetition. Few of them have intentionally been designed or created to be efficient or help you save time. But have you really paused a second to think: "Am I doing all this in the best possible way possible? Are my activities and method of working saving me time or just squeezing out the very little time I have?" That's what BPR aims to do - to reengineer your day-to-day activities from scratch, with productivity and efficiency as your focus, rather than just getting through your day. Through this chapter, we will make your stream faster and more efficient. So, let's get reengineering!

-Efficiency is doing better what is already being done.
-Peter.F.Drucker

Just a Little!

So, the question that arises now is - what are the activities that can be reengineered? If you are like me and believe nothing is 100% perfect and there is always room to improve, ALL the activities you do in a day might be altered to increase its efficiency by just a little. Brush your teeth just a little faster, finish your chores just a little faster, assign someone to do your mindless tasks so you can gain just a little time. "Just a little" from many activities will accumulate and you can find time you never knew you had. But how do you know if the work is being done efficiently?

This is done through a process known as "time and motion study." Take any of the hundreds of activities you do each day; it could be something as simple as brushing your teeth or something as complex as making strategies for your business. Now, estimate the time you would require to finish the work if you worked at your maximum productivity. Once you've done that, start the work and keep a track on time.

Did you complete the work within the time you estimated? If not, the process needs re-engineering.

Through BPR, your aim is to be as efficient as possible doing the tasks you do every day. Tasks that have become such a deep part of you that you don't stop to judge them. Simplify your activities and streamline them to minimize movement to the maximum. To illustrate with an example, the other day, I was in the office sending out a few couriers. I had to fold 63 letters, put them in envelopes, and seal it before handing them over. To streamline the process as much as possible and remove unnecessary movements, I placed all the letters on the right and all the envelopes on the left, then I just put both together in one swoosh and pushed it upwards. It didn't take long to complete 63. Another instance is when I was writing this book. I had all the information I had to put into each chapter on a paper next to me. I had a hard copy of the outline right next to the computer; this way, I didn't spend time searching or even switching tabs to find the information while I was typing. You need to train your brain to look for the easiest and most efficient ways to do any task. Remember, it might not be much time when taken individually, but when put together, it could be in hours.

-Efficiency is intelligent laziness.
-David Dunham

While there is no set step by step procedure you can use to re-engineer every task, here are a few principles you can apply to make your tasks more efficient

Let's Get Reengineering!

Do it now!

Tasks are often blown up way more than intended. How much time does it take to take out the garbage? How much time does it take to call your boss and let him know you won't be coming? How much time does it take to fold your sheets after you wake up? How much time does it take to archive unnecessary mail the moment you read it? These small tasks, which could have been done in a few seconds if you didn't put them away for later, pile up on each other to create a whole world of responsibilities and pending tasks. You now have to allocate time for the small tasks as you reluctantly go through all of them.

This was the case with my friend Sid. He spends a good hour of his evening cleaning things up. I had only one question for him: "How did the mess come up in the first place?" Do you know why? - Because Sid procrastinated his small chores and gave them more meaning than they deserve. He brings clothes from the laundry and drops them right on the bed, instead of putting them in the drawer. He comes home from work and drops his bag in a corner and shoes in another to throw himself in the couch. He eats and leaves his plate on the table, instead of taking a minute to clean it and put it back onto the shelf. He wakes up every morning and goes to the bathroom, instead of folding the blanket first. This continues until he has no choice but spend an hour cleaning everything. How many of you are guilty of the same mistakes that Sid makes?

-If it can be done in less than 2 minutes, do it now!
-David Allen

Tasks that can be done in just a few minutes will take more time if procrastinated, as you have to "find" time to do them later. You now have to allocate precious time to doing things that didn't have to come up in the first place. If any task takes less than a few minutes, say 2 or 3 minutes, "do it now"! You will be surprised by the sheer number of tasks you can knock off your to-do list by following this small process. Sid never learnt this, but I am sure you will!

Sharpen your skills

A blunt axe could cut down a mighty tree, but the sharp axe would've started chopping the next tree by then. Like a bird who rubs his beaks on tree branches to keep it sharp and clean, keeping your skill set sharp and clean is just as important to catch the worm in time.

A janitor or a CEO, every task has a basic skill requirement. Keeping them sharp and ready at call is critical to doing tasks fast. As I said, you can get through a task without having the required level of skill but not in a very efficient way. Are you a writer? - Learn to touch type even before you start your first article. Are you a chef? - Learn to cut and clean food efficiently before you start cooking. Are you a professional? - Learn to recall your laws and regulations within seconds. Do you read a lot? - Learn to speed read before you read your next book. Do you work a lot on the computer? - Learn all the shortcuts and hotkeys before you work on your next document. Are you learning the guitar? - Get your scales right before you tackle that solo.

Learning these skills can reduce the "time demand" of your tasks. Find the skill that can help you reduce the time demand of your tasks and master it before you get to work.

Manage Time leaks

Have you ever had a dripping tap at home? Those taps that keep dripping all night that we never care to repair as the wastage is so little? The next time you see one, leave a tumbler under it and see the result the next morning. You would be surprised to see the tumbler filled by just the small drops from the tap. You can only imagine the water that a small leak can waste if left unattended. It might not be much now, but it accumulates to be much more than we expect.

The same goes with time. All of us have a few leaking taps in our schedule. Allow me to quote a few - Do you watch Television? Do you wake up and sit groggy in your bed for some time before you get out of bed? Do you often get distracted by people in your workplace? Do you get up often from your workplace to go get the files you require? Do you check your phone often while studying? These are the leaking taps in your schedule. Time leaks are minute amounts of time that get wasted while you are doing your regular activities. They might not be significant at the moment and can easily slip through without you even noticing, but try putting all of it together, and you will be shocked by the time that gets wasted.

15 minutes of commercials are broadcasted for an hour-long show. So, if you watch a 3-hour movie on TV, you just wasted 45 minutes of your precious time. Research has shown an average employee spends well over 1.5 hours searching for files and distracted by fellow workers. These might not seem much when it happens, but put all of them together and you will be surprised. We are so used to doing things that way we miss the time actually wasted on these activities.

Instead of watching a movie with all the commercials on television, why not buy the movie and watch undisturbed? Jump out of bed immediately after you wake up; not only does this save time, but it also helps you get rid of laziness. Keep away all the distractions while you are working, mute your phone, put up a sign that reads do-not-disturb on your door. Don't waste time talking to colleagues during work time. Keep all your necessary work documents within an arm's length before you sit at your workplace. This ensures you don't have to get up every time you need a file; reduce movement as much as possible. Trim the excess from your activities and make them efficient.

When all of us are running in a world with constant shortage of time, you really should not be allowing small leaks to rob you of your time. Take time and assess all such activities you have in your schedule and plug them in time!

> *-Identify the essential. Eliminate the rest.*
> *-Leo Babauta*

Create a sense of urgency

I cannot get through this topic without quoting the famous example of the night before an exam or a report submission. So, let's get that out of the way before we get into the discussion. I am sure all of you have experienced the stress and tension of those last few hours before the deadline! Those dreadful nights of sleeplessness and constant stress with the regret of not starting earlier! We don't sleep, we don't eat, we don't lift our heads from the table. The work must be completed on time. That's all that matters! We hustle and rush and take care of each minute. Ah! Not really an experience to cherish, is it? But there's one thing you can take home from those horrid nights - the level of productivity you achieve! Even though out of compulsion, you work beyond what you've ever worked your entire life. You do things quickly; you want them finished as fast as possible.

> *-Nothing says work efficiency like panic mode.*
> *-Don Roff*

Now, how would your work be if you had worked the same way from the first day? How much better could you have finished your work if you worked with a sense of urgency from the first day of the project? Wouldn't your project be complete? Would you have time to spare after you completed your project? That is what I want you to learn from this part of the chapter - inculcate a habit of working with a sense of urgency!

Go through all your daily activities just a little faster. Brush your teeth a little faster, finish your chores a little faster, finish your work a little faster; make it a habit to work with a constant sense of urgency. As I have told throughout the chapter, the "just a little" will accumulate to give you a large block of empty time. Doing your tasks faster than your traditional method of working could be unnatural initially. But stick to it until it becomes a habit and you become a person who does his work fast. A slight sense of urgency can save you quite a lot of time but take care not to overdo it.

Now that you've learnt all about BPR, get busy applying it. The list of methods to re-engineer is only limited by your imagination. If I can re-engineer the task of putting letters in covers, I am sure you can do miracles with it!

Everyone would love to hear the tasks you reengineered in your day.

Click here to share it with fellow TMSers

Or go to http://bit.ly/TMSgroup

TMS ingredients in this chapter:

1. *Apply Reengineering to every activity you do regularly.*

2. *Identify tasks that need reengineering by timing them.*

3. *Apply various principles and reengineer it with efficiency being your priority.*

Chapter 8

Relax and Have Fun: Create a Fun Stream

Ralph has one last story for us, perhaps the most meaningful of them all.

Ralph and his wife loved apples. They ate their hearts out on freshly picked red apples. Even though they couldn't afford the costlier variety of apples, they saved up to buy and savour them. One day, Ralph came up with an idea - "Why don't we get an apple tree? There's plenty of room in the backyard! No shed or well to fight our tree here eh!" For the first time in his life, Ralph had come up with a good idea; with a sense of pride, his wife agreed to it.

The next day, Ralph brought home the brightest looking apple sapling he could get his hands on; he found a good spot in the yard and planted it firmly in the ground. His eyes gleamed with the dreams he had for the sapling.

"Ah! This tree is going to fill up with bright juicy apples soon," he said to his wife. "Can you even dream about the money we are going to make from selling the extra ones? We could sit under the tree all day munching fresh apples as we watch the sun set bright and orange. Our grandchildren can tie ropes and play on the tree branches one day. We've done a great thing today, my love. We've done a great thing!"

The sapling was in the right hands; it was tended to and loved like a child of the house. The couple watered and nurtured it better than they had fed their own children. "It is growing! It will meet all my dreams, ha! I will be the proudest man in town; it will be a good show for those jealous neighbours, too," he would often say to his wife as they tended to the plant.

Years passed this way and the tree looked promising. It had become a smart young tree with all its glorious leaves and short branches. Ralph's wife would often ask him to spend time with her under the tree in the evenings, just as he had dreamed.

"That one? You want me to spend time with you under that thing you call a tree? It still has a long way to go to become a tree. People would call us mad! Have patience, my love. Haven't you heard great people say, 'patience is virtue' or something like that. All in good time, my love; all in good time."

The tree was doing outstandingly well, but the same could not be said about Ralph's wife's health. She caught a flu and was bedridden for months. The poor soul couldn't take the suffering for long. She passed on peacefully in her sleep one night.....

The poor old man was shaken, but he didn't lose hope on the tree. He tended it with even more heart now. He wanted the tree to be a memory of his wife and their gift to the grandchildren. A few more years passed this way until one day the tree flowered. The tree filled with white and pink flowers. Ralph watched the tree with a sense of pride with tear-filled eyes. His grandchildren jumped with happiness seeing the number of flowers on the tree.

"Oh Grandpa! Could we have a few flowers?" the children asked with their large glistening eyes.

"Huh! You pick a flower and you lose an apple. Which do you want? The apple or the flower?" Ralph replied coldly.

Within a few days, the flowers turned to fruits. The tree was filling up with tiny apples. The kids were the first to notice it in the morning. They jumped of joy and ran inside to show it to their grandpa. They went to his room to wake him up. They screamed and shouted their lungs out to wake him up. But he just didn't.......

What's your take on the story? Do you think Ralph succeeded in life? Let's discuss.....

-You only live once but if you do it right, once is enough.
-Mae West

Pursuit of Success

In our run for success, we often miss the little things in life that make more sense than the project you have to complete or the sales graph you have to double. We get so obsessed with our work we do not give time to the things that matter. We are so focused on reaching the "garden with a thousand flowers" that we do not stop to smell the flowers on the way. The flowers in the garden might be sweeter smelling than the ones on its path, but a dried up rose you picked up on the way can be more meaningful than a thousand roses of luxury and success. Life isn't cruel. It throws a few flowers at us on our way to the garden. We should decide whether to stop and enjoy the flower or stomp over it to reach the garden with many more flowers.

- It is the time you have wasted for your rose that makes your rose so important

- Antoine de Saint-Exupéry

Enjoy the Process

We often postpone our lives, just like Ralph did. All of us have a limited time on this lovely planet. Why not make it the best you can imagine? Only if Ralph knew this! He would've made it a point to enjoy the sunset with what is available, to enjoy seeing the tree grow, to gift and give whenever possible, even if things aren't the way he wanted it to be. We want things to be perfect before we start enjoying things. We want to finish our work before we do what we love to do. We want to be rich and successful to enjoy life but many do not realize life works the other way around. Success is simply a destination of life or as I said, the garden with a thousand flowers; it's the journey to the garden that makes the success worthwhile. Finishing a task can't give you happiness if you did not enjoy getting there. The memories of your struggle and the small moments of happiness you spent with your loved ones could be your biggest wealth in life - the dried rose.

-In the end it's not the years in your life that count. It's the life in your years.

-Abraham Lincoln

You may have to postpone your happy moments by a few days to finish something you are working on and that's fine, but don't forget to come back to life stronger than ever when it's over. Spend time with your loved ones, make friends, travel to places, don't give up on your passion and hobbies, and, most importantly, have fun and make memories with whatever you have in life. A thousand flowers can't make you happy if you do not know to enjoy the smell of a flower. Learn to enjoy the small moments in life, appreciate them, and find happiness in them. If you wait for big moments to make you happy, you wouldn't have many to quote. Life is a train of small happy moments with a few chunks of huge happy moments. Find happiness in small things such as - helping your clients in business, being able to live another day, helping people find solutions, cooking something for your family, reading this book, learning something new etc.

-There is virtue in work and there is virtue in rest. Use both and overlook neither.

-Alen Cohen

A rather weird thing to be saying in a time management book. Don't you think? No, I haven't lost track of our topic. While all the time management experts teach you to finish a lot of work and work even more, I want to say - work hard but don't miss out on life in the process! Like I said, my aim is to create a lifelong system for you to follow, not just a method of working productively. A good TMS should contain enough happiness and color, or you won't be able to sustain it throughout your life. Even if you manage to create a TMS without fun and color, you would lead a miserable life and that is not something I teach. This is the greatest message I want you to take home through this book - *Time management is a method to live life to the fullest, not to work even more than what you are already doing.*

When was your last vacation? Where did you go? I'm sure everyone would love to hear it.

Click here and share it with us

Or go to http://bit.ly/TMSgroup

I Hate My Job!

How much work do you have pending? Since you are reading this book and have made it this far, I assume you have a lot pending. But don't we all have it? Every time we work on a project, we start determined; we have a dream of finishing the whole work in a few hours to get back home with the satisfaction of a finished task in our bags. But things don't like to go the way we want it to go. A task you estimated to finish in a day often goes on for 3 or 4 days and things creep into your "pending items" list. I am sure you can relate. I have to confess I am an "expert" in underestimating my tasks and having loads of work pending.

"How much more time until the book is complete?"

"Yeah, just a few more days and you will be getting your copy."

I remember telling this 6 months ago! I have been hiding from that friend ever since. I am sure she is waiting for her copy when I am only halfway through the writing.

Sometimes, things can blow up way more than we expected, and at other times, your work just doesn't seem to finish. You work without a break but work seems miles from completion. You get frustrated, feel guilty, and beat yourself up for not completing the work. Even though the work is not urgent, you feel disheartened and promise to finish the task before you do anything else. In a scenario like this, what would you normally do? You pick up your phone and cancel the dinner plan you had or you ask your friends to go on without you. You let your work life take over your personal life, and you end up with a life with no real work life balance.

So, what is the real problem here? Not the work load, not the lack of time, but something that I call "dissatisfaction in yourself." We lack the ability to appreciate ourselves and be satisfied with the work we complete. We find satisfaction only on finishing a task and not in making progress towards completion. Some tasks naturally need time to finish. You need to be patient and enjoy the process. Let me bring back the book writing example to clarify things. There are people out there who can finish a book in just 24 hours, where I took half a year to complete this book! If I am not satisfied with the work I completed, I would soon put myself in unnecessary pressure and stress.

Before we learn how you can be satisfied with your work, let's understand how your brain works to make you feel satisfied. Your brain has evolved in such a way it repeats the things you like and avoid the things you find less pleasurable. Good food, music, exercise, and other such activities releases a neurotransmitter known as dopamine in your brains; this leaves you happy and makes you crave more of the activity. The same way, when you complete a task, your brain produces dopamine, which gives you the feeling of accomplishment and happiness, which motivates you to work harder. Your brain only produces dopamine when the work is "complete", not when the work is half done. This causes the dissatisfaction of incomplete tasks. If you continue to beat yourself up and work harder than before, it won't be long before you lose all your motivation and resent the task. This is when you find yourself saying: "God! I hate my job!" You skip the pleasurable activities of your day to make way for the pending work. This way, your personal life takes a dip and you lose your work life balance.

Dissatisfaction in yourself - the biggest reason for lack of work life balance. Now that you know the working of your brain, it is simple to find a solution for this problem - be satisfied with the work you completed. See the glass as half full, instead of half empty! I would still appreciate and feel proud of myself if I wrote just one line a day. This way, I associate pleasure and happiness to my work, which drives me to work harder the next day, instead of feeling disheartened and beating myself up for not being on track.

The truth is your work will never be done. There will always be tasks pending and things you have to do. You can't let this get in the way of your personal life. Stop working when your feel you have worked enough; don't try to finish the whole task in one day. Knowing when to stop is vital to keeping a healthy personal life. As we saw before, being satisfied is important not only to keep a balance in your work and life, but also to help you work better and stay motivated when you complete your important tasks. Acknowledge and appreciate yourself and your mind will reward you handsomely.

-Rest and be thankful.

-William Wadsworth

TMS ingredients in this chapter:

1. *Appreciate and be content with life no matter where you are in life.*
2. *Be satisfied with the work you complete no matter how little it may be.*
3. *Don't beat yourself up beyond what is possible.*
4. *Maintain a good work life balance.*

The TMS Action Sheet

The Whole Picture

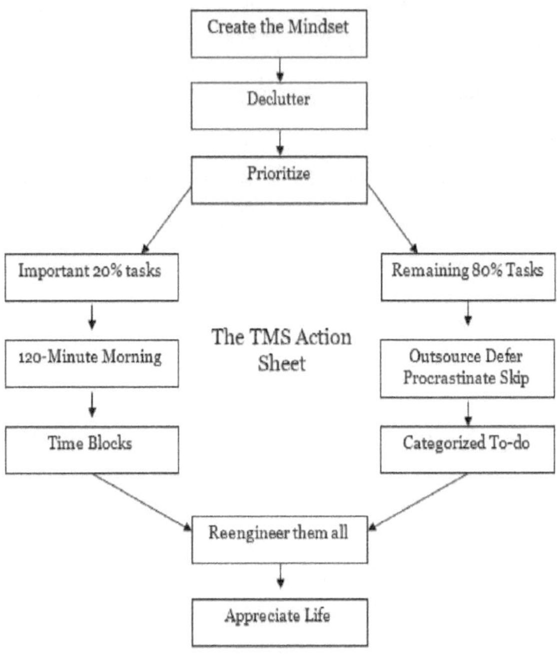

Here is an action list to make sure you apply the TMS in your life. I know it is nowhere as comprehensive as the whole book, but it can help you in getting things running. Head over to the Facebook group if you want a print ready version. It could make an excellent reminder on your workplace until the TMS becomes a habit.

Click here and find the PDF version on the Facebook group

Or go to http://bit.ly/TMSgroup

The Recipe

Every time I read a book, I have this fear that I might forget some of the valuable information the book has to offer and end up losing a life changing opportunity. That will not be the case with this book, here is the summary of all the 24 ingredients that make the first part of the book:

1. *Make the TMS an everlasting habit.*
2. *Conserve every minute of your day with the investment mentality.*
3. *Be in a good state at all times by keeping your mind and body in top condition.*
4. *Practice the two-minute fix every time you feel low.*
5. *Be organized as it can save you a lot of mental juice.*
6. *Keep your surroundings, workplace and mind free from clutter.*
7. *Don't work hard! Start working smart by prioritizing your tasks.*
8. *Apply the Pareto's principle as a method of prioritizing. Use it to find you most important 20% tasks.*
9. *Concentrate your efforts on your most important tasks and let your other tasks take a step back.*
10. *Apply various techniques to detach from the remaining 80% tasks.*
11. *Wake up early and change the way you use your morning time.*
12. *Do a morning ritual to be in a good state of mind every day.*
13. *Work on your most important tasks first thing in the morning.*
14. *Harness the power of your superhero and exploit the first 120 minutes of each day.*
15. *Have control over your day.*
16. *Create time blocks for the important 20% tasks in your day*
17. *Use a categorized to-do list to tackle the remaining 80% tasks.*
18. *Apply Reengineering to every activity you do regularly.*
19. *Identify tasks that need reengineering by timing them.*
20. *Apply various principles and reengineer it with efficiency*

being your priority.

21. *Appreciate and be content with life no matter where you are in life.*
22. *Be satisfied with the work you complete no matter how little it may be.*
23. *Don't beat yourself up beyond what is possible.*
24. *Maintain a good work life balance*

PART II: Maintaining Your Stream

What Next?

In the first part of the book, we went into detail on how you can build your own TMS. We learnt the ingredients that make up a good day and restructured your day to form a powerful, strong daily routine. Apply all of them to your stream, and soon, you will see tremendous changes in your life. In a perfect world, it's all fine, but the world we live in is far from perfect. Obstacles and problems are bound to show up to throw your stream off-course and force it to return to the path it has been following for years. Through the second part of the book, we will stick fences and barbed wires around your stream. The TMS is a system for life, and we will make sure it stays that way no matter what comes in its path. Let's use the obstacles and problems that one would normally face in their attempt to learn time management and lead a disciplined life as reasons to better our craft and skill. Follow along, and together, we will make sure the TMS sticks throughout your life to give you all the time you never knew you had. By the end of the book, you will have a clean, swift, powerful stream, and that's my word!

Chapter 9

Laser Sharp Focus!

-The successful warrior is the average man, with laser-like focus.
-Bruce Lee

You made it this far into the book! Do I even have to teach you about focus? You have extraordinary focus, and you are determined to learn the art of time management; you have proven yourself! Well done! Let's better your amazing focus through this chapter. Give yourself a pat on your back as you continue into the chapter.

"How do you stay focused on your work? I can't work on a task for more than 10 minutes," asked Rachel, tired of not being able to complete her work on time. Rachel could never work on a task for over 10 minutes. She easily got distracted by the smallest of the small. She described the clocks got slower every time she sat down to work, and her mind will bring up incidents and pictures of everything in the world, except for the work she was supposed to be doing. She had to check her phone every few minutes, or she felt she was missing out on something important. This is a serious problem that many of us face. What benefit can schedules and time blocks be if one does not have the required focus to follow through and concentrate?

The solution to this is simple. Rachel found the solution of her problem all by herself! I just had to turn the situation in such a way she came up with the solution. She laughed, thinking why she couldn't come up with it earlier. If you have the same problem, read on and you will find the solution for it yourself.

I gave Rachel a simple story and asked her a question – What would you do if a person came up to you and said: "I want to participate in the marathon the upcoming month, but I simply cannot get my legs working. I run for 10 minutes and I have to stop for breath, I pant, and just can't help but stop running! I am not fit enough to run a marathon. The maximum time I have ever run is 15 minutes. I can't run a minute more than that."

Rachel, being the athlete she is, was quick to snap back: "He needs to practice more; he doesn't have the required stamina to run more than 15 minutes." He doesn't have enough "stamina" she said. Rachel was right; you can't expect to run a marathon if you've never run for 100 meters in your life. You need tremendous stamina to run a full marathon.

Now, the question I had is this: "Why is stamina applicable only for our physical body? Why not to our mind? After all, the brain is an organ in the body too." It was then the answer flashed!

Focus Stamina

Similar to the stamina we have for our physical activities, we have stamina for our mind, called "focus stamina." The better your focus stamina, the longer you can work. People who can work for long hours without a break are the marathon runners! They have extraordinary amounts of focus stamina! You can't work for over 10 minutes? - build up your stamina. And how do you build up your stamina? - the same way you would build your physical stamina, by pushing yourself harder.

Here's a simple exercise to help you build your focus stamina and work hours without losing motivation and productivity.

> 1)   Start where you are - What is the maximum time you can go without losing focus? Note the time, say 15 minutes.

> 2)   Increase your work time by a minute or two every day until you have reached your desired goal. It is a time-consuming process, but marathon runners aren't made in a day, are they? Be patient with it, and you will definitely appreciate the results! Continue the process gradually and within a few months, you would work hours without breaking a sweat!

Distractions Cannot Be Removed!

-Starve your distractions, feed your focus
-Unknown

Every tree sways in the wind. The strong ones stay put, while the weak ones get uprooted. In the huge world, distractions are increasing by the day. Every person must deal with distractions - the shiny things along the way that seem more important than the work, which we regret doing at the end of the day. All of us would've had to deal with them at some point of our lives.

Let me tell you a secret about distractions - they can't be removed! You read that right; removing distractions from your life is a painful procedure. It was only the other day I installed a casual game on my phone, while I waited for my turn to see the doctor. Unfortunately, it didn't stop there. It turned out to be a huge addiction brutally eating into all my time with no hint of mercy. Now, the traditional solution to distractions are simple - remove them, *but how?* You need a world of self-discipline to stop checking your phone every few minutes, to not go online the moment you get a few seconds.

Before we get into the discussion, I want to narrate an incident that happened to me the other day. I was attending a family function, and like every other family gathering, I naturally lost track of time. Even though it was late, eventually, I checked on my watch and was shocked to notice it was way past the time I intended to leave. I quickly packed up my bag and waved everyone goodbye, but I just couldn't find my car keys! Not until I found my cute two-year-old niece playing with them. She had developed quite a liking towards my fancy jingling keychain and insisted she keep it when I was on my toes - ready to run out. I pleaded and pleaded, but she just kept running away with my keys every time I asked her. You could only imagine how awkward the situation got! This was when my sister brought out a big shiny chocolate wrapped in a golden cover and gave it to the kid. The kid's eyes gleamed with happiness! She dropped the keys right where she was standing and went on happily asking someone to open the chocolate bar for her, when I stood there embarrassed at my skill with kids.

The kid willingly surrendered the keys for a bar of shiny chocolate when all my techniques of trying to plead with her failed. I know I am bad with kids, but my sister had done so easily what I couldn't do with much effort! The same goes with distractions! Removing distractions can be a tedious task, but replacing them is not! That's the secret! That's the right way to handle a distraction - *replace it!* Going back to my example of the game on my phone - I replaced the game on my phone with an audiobook application. Every time I felt bored or thought of checking on my villagers in the game, I would simply open the app and listen to a good book. Do you have a habit of opening your phone every 10 minutes? Get a watch to check time. Do you waste a lot of time on social media? Interact with the people around you every time you feel the urge to check your notifications. Are TV shows eating into your time? Fix a time block of exercising at the exact time the show airs. Making the replacement more attractive than the distraction itself is a good idea. Make your mind crave the replacement, instead of the distraction.

Another amazing way to get rid of distractions is to language them differently. We already learnt the power of languaging your thoughts in chapter #2 <u>Mindset: Dig a New Path</u>. Language your mind to find the negatives of the distractions. A few months back, I found myself watching too much of a TV series. Do you know how I stopped watching it? - I found faults in the characters. Every time the character did something, I would think in my mind - "really? Is that how you handle a situation? The character is not a person I would make friends with." I continued doing this until my mind perceived the TV series as a negative thing. Yeah, I know I was being picky and unfair, but we need to protect our time, and that is more important.

> *-Temporary pain leads to permanent pleasure, temporary pleasure lead to permanent pain.*
> *-My Teacher*

What did you replace your distractions with? The group could use some creative attacks against distractions.

<u>Click here and let's tackle them together</u>

Or go to <u>http://bit.ly/TMSgroup</u>

Two Letters to Save You Hours

Two letters that can save you hours a day? Is that even possible? Or is it simply a catchy title? Once I started applying this, I had so much time in hand I had to rewrite all my time blocks to extend the time I spend on each. I got a feeling I was in charge of my life and that relieved a ton of stress and pressure. I was confident I have enough time to achieve all I wished to achieve each day. But all this with just two letters?

NO! - That's the magical word! Warren Buffet, one of the wealthiest men on the face of the earth, once said: *"The difference between successful people and very successful people is that very successful people **say no** to almost everything."* Often, we say yes to everything - the dinner with family, the lunch with friends, the lecture at the university, the meeting with your boss etc. We don't realize these appointments are like boats in the horizon. You look at the boat far off in the distance and say: "What a small boat, it will fit anywhere." But it is not until it reaches the port you realize the boat was not a boat but a massive 60,000-ton ship. We say yes to the boat in the horizon and not the ship at the port. We think to ourselves: "It is only a half an hour meeting. I will make it," and when the day of the meeting arrives, you have 6 other meetings, a doctor's appointment, your son's graduation, and you lose your car keys. Now, you realize the size of the ship and reluctantly cancel the previously scheduled meeting and end up with only regret and stress to accompany you. A better way to handle a situation like this? – Don't overcommit from the start.

-It's only by saying "NO" that you can concentrate on the things that are really important.

-Steve Jobs

If your colleagues ask you to go out to with dinner with them, tell them "I will try my best to be there, but I am working on an important project that might keep me busy," rather than just a plain old, "yeah, I'll try." Say "yes" only to the things that matter to you. Be conservative in giving your time to others. Unless you are sure you want to be someplace, never say "yes." Try it. You will be surprised by the amount of time you can save. But a word of caution - be diplomatic when you say "no." You don't want to end up with strained relationships and broken friendships just because you say "no" a lot.

-If something is not a "hell, YEAH!", then it's a "no!"
-James Altucher

Chapter 10

A Gold Mine?

Now that you have a strong foundation of time management, every tip or time management trick you come across can be a nugget of gold. Like I promised in the beginning of the book, time management tips and tricks will have a new meaning, once you have a TMS in place – they become the caretakers of your stream. Now that you know all the ingredients of the TMS, I urge you to put it into practice and strengthen them with a few tips and tricks. So, let's dive into the gold mine of knowledge. Here are 11 short golden nuggets to shoot your time management skills through the roof.

The 11 Golden Nuggets

1) Procrastination

"Let's do it tomorrow" - what an amazing idea until it's tomorrow already! The age-old problem that needs no introduction - procrastination! You would expect procrastination to have its own chapter in a book on time management, but procrastination does not exist in my life and you know why? - I have a solid TMS in place. Follow all the principles of the TMS, and you will soon forget to procrastinate. Procrastination has one big root; chop it off and procrastination cannot survive.

-Procrastination is a symptom and not a disease.

-Unknown.

Temporal Discounting is that root! It is the tendency of the mind to give greater value to rewards in the present than rewards in the future. We prefer short-term pleasures to bigger, better rewards in the future. This is something that can be cured easily. A person with a solid TMS can easily combat procrastination with techniques such as prioritizing, eating a frog, scheduling etc. Procrastination can only exist when there is lack of clarity. When things are crystal clear, your mind knows exactly what it's expected to do; there is no way you can find room for procrastination in your life. You are in a productive state and procrastination? – forgotten forever!

2) Never be late again.

There's one weird thing about being late or missing your train or flight. "You almost made it!" The train always leaves a few seconds before you could get to the station, your boss always arrives a few seconds before you could enter the door, the meeting always starts a few seconds before you could get in! This trick I have for you will make sure you are never late again. Set all the clocks around you to be 5 minutes faster, forget you did it, and that's it! A neat trick to be 5 minutes early to every appointment. Try it, it works!

3) Another Clock Trick

I am more of a morning person, and I hate working late hours. The moment the clock ticks 10, my brain shuts down. I lose all my sense of creativity and motivation, but sometimes, you can't afford to go to bed so early. My friend Ricky gave me a small work-around to tackle this time driven problem of mine; he asked me to change my table clock's time to 6pm every time I have to work beyond 10pm. Your brain is not very smart; you can fool it easily. Even though my conscious mind knows it's well past 10, your subconscious mind works as though it is only 6pm. A definite trick to try!

4) Burnouts

We discussed in the first part of the book that willpower is an exhaustible resource. I look at willpower as a small pond of water; you can use it all you want, and it keeps replenishing itself until those few months when drought hits! The strong heat dries up all the water, leaving the pond unable to replenish itself. This is when the pond requires a good amount of refreshing rainfall! A few days of good rainfall and the pond is filled with crystal clear water again.

The same goes with our willpower, there are times of heavy pressure and stress when our pond dries up. In such situations of drought, it cannot self-regenerate; it requires a good amount of rainfall! If you ever feel like you cannot get motivated to work or work productively no matter what you try, it is a clear sign you are experiencing burnout! Only a good long vacation can bring the dead pond back to life!

You can avoid such a drought by properly scheduling breaks into your TMS. Regular rainfall is better than a heavy rain after the damage has already been done.

5) Energy

A car is made to take you places fast, but when it runs out of fuel, it becomes a burden as you have to tow it to the next fuel station or travel further than your original destination to get fuel for it. Similarly, a TMS without energy is a car without fuel; it becomes a burden, rather than helping you reach places. It is hard to follow schedules and create habits when you lack the energy to do so. We will learn about the components of energy in the following points.

6) The most common reason for fatigue

CBS reports up to 75% of the American population falls short of the daily 10 cups of water intake. Dehydration is the main reason of fatigue in most people, and it is the most neglected too. Keep your body well-hydrated and you will bubble with energy! Drinking green juices and other fruit juices is my favorite method of staying hydrated. Judging your urine color is the best way to find out if you are well-hydrated. Ideally, it should be colorless or pale yellow. If not – gulp down a huge glass of water.

7) Don't need an alarm!

With the constant shortage of time, sleep has become more of a luxury than a necessity. While sleep timings can vary from person to person, a minimum of 6-7 hours of sleep is a necessity for human beings to work at their peak levels of attention and concentration. Sleep deficit can build up and lead to bigger problems than low productivity, such as high risk of obesity, diabetes, and permanent damage to the brain.

Sleeping 7 hours alone is not sufficient; your TMS should be made in such a way it allows you to sleep and wake up at the same time every day. Allow me to explain a little about sleep cycles to drive home my point. While we sleep, our body goes through five stages of sleep in repetitive cycles with each cycle lasting about 90 minutes. The deeper the stage of sleep you wake up from, the more tired and groggy you will be when you are awake. To help you with this waking up process, your biological clock reduces the intensity of these cycles as you near your normal wake up time, ultimately reducing the willpower required to get out of bed. But if you follow no regular sleep pattern, there is no way your body can estimate the time of your sleep when it has to reduce the intensity of the sleep cycles, not until an alarm wakes you up from the deepest phase of your sleep, leaving you ever so tired and sleepier than what you were when you got into bed.

Your body loves predictability and creating a habit of sleeping and waking up at the same time every day not only can boost your productivity levels, but also help you wake up easier. Do this for a consistent number of days and you will have created a habit of waking up at a specific time with no alarm. I never use an alarm clock, unless I have to wake up at 3 in the morning to pick up my friend from the airport.

8) Music

Tried working with music? Research says music can boost productivity. I love listening to classical music with no lyrics when I work! I owe Ludovico Einaudi's a lot! His music kept me going and creatively bubbly when I wrote this book.

9) Pomodoro Technique

The Pomodoro technique emphasises the importance of breaks in your routine. It says - Work 25 minutes and take a break of 5 minutes. This keeps the brain fresh and rejuvenated. I would quote this technique as only a place to start, rather than the goal. It's an excellent way to build your focus stamina. I remember having used this technique extensively with constantly increasing time when I was still in college. I started at the traditional 25/5 minutes' ratio and kept increasing the work and break time until I found my own sweet ratio of 90 minutes of work and 30 minutes of break. I find taking

www.ingramcontent.com/pod-product-compliance
Lightning Source LLC
Chambersburg PA
CBHW020503160726
47991CB00007B/2786